Built for Speed

The World's Fastest Pro Stock Trucks

by Jeff Savage

CAPSTONE
HIGH-INTEREST
BOOKS

an imprint of Capstone Press
Mankato, Minnesota

Capstone High-Interest Books are published by Capstone Press
151 Good Counsel Drive, P.O. Box 669, Mankato, Minnesota 56002
http://www.capstone-press.com

Library of Congress Cataloging-in-Publication Data
Savage, Jeff, 1961–
 The World's fastest pro stock trucks/by Jeff Savage.
 p. cm.—(Built for speed)
 Summary: Describes the design, safety features, and professional racing
of stock trucks, which are ultrapowered versions of American-built pickup
trucks.
 Includes bibliographical references and index.
 ISBN 0-7368-1502-3 (hardcover)
 1. Trucks—Juvenile literature. 2. Truck racing—Juvenile literature.
[1. Trucks. 2. Truck racing.] I. Title. II. Series: Built for speed (Mankato,
Minn.)
TL230.15 .S283 2003
796.7—dc21   2002012619

**Capstone Press thanks NASCAR's Owen Kearns for his help in preparing
this book.**

Editorial Credits
Matt Doeden, editor; Karen Risch, product planning editor; Timothy Halldin,
 series designer; Patrick Dentinger, book designer; Jo Miller, photo researcher

Photo Credits
AP/Wide World Photos/Ed Reinke, 16
Courtesy Craftsman Truck Series, 23, 25
Getty Images/Jamie Squire, cover, 27, 36, 43; Robert Laberge, 4, 8, 10, 19, 32, 34;
 David Taylor, 7, 40; Jonathan Ferrey, 13, 14, 31, 35; Darrell Ingham, 20–21;
 Chris Stanford, 26; Donald Miralle, 28; Craig Jones, 38

1 2 3 4 5 6 08 07 06 05 04 03

Table of Contents

Chapter 1

NASCAR
Craftsman Trucks

Thirty-six colorful trucks form two long rows behind a pace truck as they circle an oval track. More than 80,000 fans stand and cheer as the pace truck enters the pits. The flagman waves a green flag to signal the start of the NASCAR Craftsman Truck Series race.

The drivers accelerate to more than 80 miles (130 kilometers) per hour as they enter the first turn. As they complete the turn, engines roar as the drivers speed up again. The trucks reach speeds of more than 180 miles (290 kilometers) per hour as they race down the backstretch.

A flagman waves a green flag to start a NASCAR Craftsman Truck Series race.

Drivers stomp on their gas pedals as they try to pass each other. One driver near the front of the group tries to pass on the outside part of the track. The truck brushes the concrete wall. Its rear end swings back and forth. The other trucks speed by as the driver slows down to regain control. The driver steps on the gas pedal again and tries to catch up to the rest of the trucks. Less than one lap of the race is complete. The drivers have another 150 laps to go.

About Craftsman Trucks

NASCAR trucks are highly tuned trucks designed to race on paved tracks. Drivers take part in NASCAR's Craftsman Truck Series. Their trucks are called Craftsman trucks.

Craftsman trucks are based on standard two-door pickup trucks. Race teams modify these pickups to perform at very high levels. They make changes to both the engine and the body of the truck to help drivers reach the highest possible speeds.

Craftsman trucks are designed to race on paved tracks.

All Craftsman trucks are built in the United States. The three main truck makers are Dodge, Ford, and Chevrolet. Race teams can choose from the top truck models made by these companies. In 2002, the top models were the Dodge Ram C-1500, the Chevrolet Silverado C-1500, and the Ford F-150.

Craftsman truck racing is based on stock car racing. Truck races have the same basic setup and rules that stock car races have. Many truck drivers get their start as stock car drivers.

Racing teams may spend millions of dollars each year to buy and modify their trucks. They earn some of this money by taking part in races. Racing teams also earn money from sponsors. Sponsors are companies that pay racing teams to promote their products. For example, an auto parts company may pay a team to place its company logo on the side of the team's truck.

Sponsors pay teams to place company logos on their trucks.

Chapter 2

The History of Craftsman Trucks

In the 1990s, stock car racing quickly grew in popularity. NASCAR had two series of stock car races, the Winston Cup Series and the Busch Series, Grand National Division. NASCAR officials wanted to promote another series of races. In 1995, they created a series of truck races.

The Origin of NASCAR
Stock car racing first became popular in the southern United States during the 1930s and 1940s. Each race had different rules.

Craftsman truck racing is based on NASCAR's popular stock car racing series.

Drivers and fans were often confused about the rules of the sport.

In 1947, driver and race promoter Bill France arranged a meeting in Daytona Beach, Florida. France invited 35 other drivers and race promoters. Together, they created a group called the National Association for Stock Car Auto Racing (NASCAR). NASCAR's goal was to set rules for all stock car races in the United States. The group members elected Bill France to serve as NASCAR's first president.

The popularity of stock car racing grew after NASCAR formed. Large paved tracks such as Daytona International Speedway were built. Soon, fans could watch NASCAR races on TV. NASCAR quickly became one of the biggest sports organizations in the world.

Truck Racing Begins

The idea for NASCAR truck racing began in 1994. The president of NASCAR at the time was Bill France Jr. Several owners of off-road racing trucks set up a meeting with France.

Darrell Waltrip is one of many racing stars to drive in NASCAR's truck races.

Off-road trucks race on dirt and mud courses. The truck owners told France that their trucks could be changed to race on paved tracks. France liked the idea.

One year later, NASCAR began its first series of truck races. NASCAR held 20 races

Mike Skinner won NASCAR's first truck racing title in 1995.

at tracks throughout the United States. Darrell Waltrip, Terry Labonte, Geoffrey Bodine, and Ken Schrader were among the NASCAR stars who took part in these early races. Mike Skinner won eight of the races and earned more than $400,000 in prize money. Skinner later became a Winston Cup driver.

Rob MacCachren, Dave Ashley, Walker Evans, and other off-road racing stars also took part in the first season of truck racing. But the off-road drivers did not do well on the paved tracks. Most of these drivers went back to off-road racing.

After the first season, Sears became the official sponsor of the truck races. Sears sells Craftsman tools. The name of the truck racing series became the Craftsman Truck Series. It is the only professional pickup truck racing series in North America.

Chapter 3

Craftsman Truck Design

Craftsman truck racing teams start with the basic body design of a pickup truck. They strip out the passenger seats and other unneeded parts. They add roll bars and other safety features to protect drivers during crashes. Powerful engines are added to give the trucks the highest possible performance.

Engines and Horsepower
A powerful engine is the most important part of a Craftsman truck. Trucks have large, eight-cylinder internal combustion engines. Fuel burns inside the cylinders, causing

Craftsman trucks must keep the basic design of a standard pickup truck.

pistons to quickly pump up and down. This motion powers the truck.

All Craftsman trucks use cast-iron V-8 engines. The engines' eight cylinders are arranged in the shape of a "V." Every Craftsman truck engine is the same size. Engines must measure 358 cubic inches (5.7 liters) to compete in Craftsman series events.

Engine strength is measured in horsepower. Standard pickup truck engines produce about 180 horsepower. Craftsman truck engines can produce more than 700 horsepower. This extra power allows the trucks to quickly reach high speeds.

Racing teams use the same engine for practice, qualifying laps, and racing. Some teams use each engine for only one week. Team members take out an engine after it has been used. They keep the main body of the engine, which is called the block. They then rebuild a new engine around the block.

All Craftsman trucks are based on pickups built by Dodge, Ford, and Chevrolet.

Craftsman trucks have aerodynamic designs that reduce drag.

Body Design

The frame of a Craftsman truck is called the chassis. All of the truck's other parts connect to the chassis. The chassis is made of strong metals such as steel and lead. Some parts of the chassis may be made of Kevlar. This material is five times stronger than steel.

The weight of the metal chassis helps to prevent the truck from lifting off the ground at high speeds.

The outside panels of a Craftsman truck must have aerodynamic designs. These designs lower air resistance, or drag. Drag slows down moving objects. NASCAR officials make rules about what kind of changes teams can make to a truck's body. These rules prevent one truck from being much faster than another truck.

A strip of aluminum called a spoiler attaches to the back of the truck. The spoiler is shaped like an upside-down airplane wing. Air passing over the spoiler pushes down on the rear of the truck, creating downforce. Downforce improves the grip of the rear tires and helps the truck accelerate more quickly. Downforce also reduces a truck's top speed. A truck with too much downforce cannot keep up with other trucks on a track's long straightaways.

Suspension

A good suspension system is important to a truck driver. A truck's suspension system includes springs and shock absorbers. These parts absorb some of the impact of racing.

The suspension system also affects a truck's handling. A truck with a suspension setup that is too soft will lose speed easily. A truck with a suspension setup that is too hard will have a rough ride. It will also handle turns badly.

CRAFTSMAN TRUCK ADJUSTABLE SUSPENSION

Front Suspension

GREEN	Shock absorbers
BLUE	Upper and lower A-arms
BROWN	Wheel tether
YELLOW	Front sway bar
ORANGE	Coil springs
PURPLE	Front disc brakes

Rear Suspension

BLUE	Trailing arms
RED	Rear axle
ORANGE	Coil springs
YELLOW	Track bar (Panhard bar)
GRAY	Wedge bolts
GREEN	Axle chains
PURPLE	Rear disc brakes

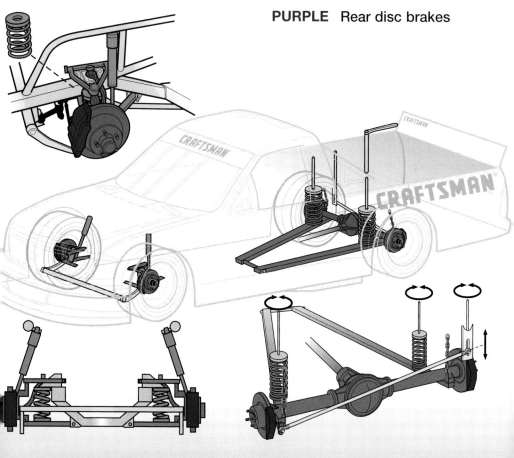

Craftsman trucks have independent suspension. The front and rear suspension systems are not connected. The front suspension includes a sway bar, which is also called an anti-roll bar. At high speeds, a truck's body will lean, or roll, into a turn. The sway bar controls the amount of body roll that a truck makes. The rear suspension includes a track bar, which controls how the truck's weight shifts during a turn. The track bar prevents the rear end of the truck from spinning out during long or sharp turns.

Safety Features

Craftsman truck racing is a dangerous sport. Even small mistakes can cause drivers to crash into walls or into other trucks. Some crashes involve 10 or more trucks. Racing teams pay close attention to the safety features of their trucks. They do everything they can to make sure the drivers are protected.

Drivers wear protective equipment and clothing during a race. They wear Kevlar helmets that protect the head and face. Their

CRAFTSMAN TRUCK SAFETY FEATURES

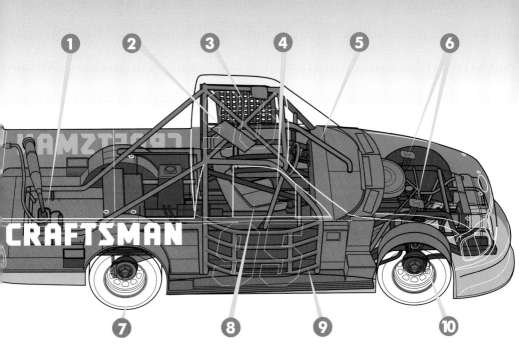

1) **Fuel tank**—lined with rubber to prevent fuel from spilling after a crash

2) **Roof flaps**—pop up to slow the truck during spins

3) **Window net**—keeps the driver's arms and head inside the truck

4) **Petty bar**—prevents the truck from collapsing during a roll

5) **Earnhardt bar**—keeps loose wheels and other objects from crashing through the windshield

6) **Hood tethers**—hold the hood tightly in place

7) **Racing slicks**—give the truck the best grip to the track surface

8) **Shaped driver's seat**—holds the driver in place during a crash

9) **Door bars**—protect the driver from a side impact

10) **Disc brakes**—provide the best stopping power

COURTESY:
CRAFTSMAN TRUCK SERIES
ARTWORK AVAILABLE AT: WWW.CARRICKPR.COM

Strong harnesses hold drivers in their seats.

full-body racing suits are made of fireproof nylon material. Even their underwear is fire-resistant.

Trucks are also designed to protect drivers. The driver's seat is made of aluminum. It fits closely around the driver's body. Drivers are strapped tightly to the seat by a safety harness.

The top of the truck is fitted with strong metal tubes called roll bars. The roll bars prevent the top of the truck from being crushed if it rolls over. Metal bars are attached to the driver's door. These bars prevent the door from smashing into the driver. Drivers also have a fire extinguisher inside the truck to put out small fires.

All of a truck's safety features protect a driver during a crash.

Chapter 4

Craftsman Truck Races

Most Craftsman truck races are held on superspeedways. These oval-shaped tracks are at least 1 mile (1.6 kilometers) long. They have banked turns that slope inward toward the center of the track. This banking helps drivers take turns at high speeds without sliding off the track. Trucks can reach speeds of more than 180 miles (290 kilometers) per hour on superspeedways.

Some races are held on short tracks. Like superspeedways, short tracks are usually oval-shaped. They are less than 1 mile (1.6 kilometers) long. Some short tracks

Superspeedways are oval-shaped tracks with long straightaways.

are less than .5 mile (.8 kilometer) long. Drivers must use their brakes to slow down more often on short tracks.

Before the Race

Drivers must run qualifying laps before they can enter a race. These timed laps decide the starting position of the trucks in the race. Drivers run qualifying laps alone. No other trucks are allowed on the track. Race officials time each driver's fastest lap. The driver with the fastest lap earns the pole position and begins the race in first place. The fastest 36 trucks qualify to take part in the race.

On race day, NASCAR officials carefully inspect each truck. They make sure that race teams have followed all of the rules. They check the engine and the fuel tank. They make sure each truck's body fits NASCAR standards. They also make sure all necessary safety gear is included.

Before the race begins, the drivers take several warm-up laps behind a pace truck.

Drivers must slow down for a short track's tight turns.

During these slow laps, they warm up the engines and the tires. Drivers often make a series of short S-shaped turns as they take warm-up laps. These turns help to heat up the tires so they grip the track.

Drivers arrange their trucks in two rows. The pole position is the spot in the first row on the inside part of the track. The second-place driver starts in the first row on the outside part of the track. The other trucks line up behind these two trucks. These two lines of trucks are called the starting grid.

The Race

A race begins when the pace truck leaves the track and a flagman waves a green flag. The drivers then speed up. Once they cross the starting line, they can leave their spots on the starting grid.

Most of a Craftsman truck race is held under a green flag. Drivers can try to pass other drivers at any time. An accident may

Drivers arrange their trucks in two long rows to start a race.

Drivers may pass each other at any time during a green flag.

change this rule. Race officials may wave a yellow flag after an accident. During a yellow flag, the pace truck returns to the track. Drivers form a grid based on their position in the race. They cannot pass one another until the pace truck leaves the track and the flagman waves a green flag again.

Pit stops are important to a racing team's success. Craftsman trucks cannot run a whole race without stopping for fuel and new tires. Their fuel tanks can hold only 22 gallons (83 liters) of fuel. Their tires wear out at high speeds. Each track has an area called the pits where drivers can stop. Teams called pit crews wait in the pits to work on their team's truck.

Trucks make pit stops for new tires and fuel.

A good pit crew can change four tires and fill the truck with fuel in about 15 seconds.

Major Events

In 2002, NASCAR held a total of 24 Craftsman Truck Series races. Many of these races are paired with Winston Cup stock car events. Truck races are held on a Friday or Saturday. Winston Cup races are usually held at the same track on the following Sunday.

Each Craftsman series race is held on a different track. The trucks race on some of the most famous tracks in North America. The most popular race of the season is held at Daytona International Speedway in Florida. This superspeedway is 2.5 miles (4 kilometers) long. Other popular tracks include the .5-mile (.8-kilometer) Martinsville Speedway in Virginia. This track is shaped like a paper clip, with very sharp turns. Darlington Raceway in South Carolina is a 1.4-mile (2.3-kilometer) egg-shaped track.

A good pit crew can can change four tires and fill a truck with fuel in about 15 seconds.

Chapter 5

Craftsman Truck Stars

Craftsman truck racing is becoming more popular every year. More than 80,000 fans have attended some races. Fans also watch the races on ESPN and other TV networks. The prize money for truck drivers has also grown. Top drivers can earn hundreds of thousands of dollars each year.

Stock Car Influence

Many of today's top truck drivers started out as stock car drivers. Some drivers, such as Jason Leffler, switched from the Winston Cup Series.

Greg Biffle and many other past Craftsman Truck Series stars have moved on to stock car racing.

They wanted to improve their racing skills. Other drivers, such as Ted Musgrave, spent years racing stock cars before deciding they wanted a change.

Some of stock car racing's biggest stars have driven in Craftsman series races. Busch Series star Jack Sprague won three Craftsman series titles in the late 1990s and early 2000s. Kevin Harvick won Winston Cup's Rookie of the Year award in 2000 after racing trucks full time from 1997 until 1999. Harvick still takes part in some Craftsman series races. Greg Biffle won the Craftsman series title in 2000. In 2001, Biffle switched to the Busch Series and was named Rookie of the Year. Tony Stewart has also driven in Craftsman events.

In 2002, racing legend Darrell Waltrip drove in several Craftsman series races. Waltrip had not raced in a NASCAR event since he retired from the Winston Cup Series in 2000.

Jack Sprague won three Craftsman Truck Series titles in the late 1990s and early 2000s.

Today's Craftsman Truck Stars

The Craftsman Truck Series does not have as many big stars as the stock car racing series. But some drivers have gained popularity in the sport.

Ted Musgrave started racing trucks in 2001 after spending 11 years racing stock cars. Musgrave had engine trouble in his first race and finished 22nd. But he then won three of the next four races. He went on to win four more races during the season and finished second in the points standings. Musgrave continued his success in 2002 by finishing in the top 10 in eight of the first 11 races.

Ron Hornaday Jr. is among the most successful Craftsman truck drivers. He won the Craftsman series title in 1996 and 1998 before switching to stock car racing. Hornaday still drives in some truck races and remains one of the sport's biggest stars. Hornaday, Musgrave, and other stars of the sport have helped to make truck racing one of the fastest-growing sports in the United States.

Ted Musgrave is among the top drivers in the Craftsman Truck Series today.

Words to Know

aerodynamic (air-oh-dye-NAM-ik)—designed to reduce air resistance

chassis (CHASS-ee)—the frame on which the body of a truck is built

cylinder (SIL-uhn-dur)—a hollow tube inside which a piston moves up and down to produce power in an engine

downforce (DOUN-forss)—the force of passing air pressing down on a moving vehicle

modify (MOD-uh-fye)—to change; mechanics modify the engine and body of a truck to improve its performance.

spoiler (SPOI-lur)—a winglike device attached to the back of a truck; spoilers help a truck's rear tires grip the track

To Learn More

Graham, Ian. *Super Trucks.* Fast Forward. New York: Franklin Watts, 2001.

Johnstone, Michael. *NASCAR.* The Need for Speed. Minneapolis: LernerSports, 2002.

Savage, Jeff. *The World's Fastest Stock Cars.* Built for Speed. Mankato, Minn.: Capstone Press, 2003.

Useful Addresses

**Daytona International Speedway
   Visitors Center**
1801 West International Speedway Boulevard
Daytona Beach, FL 32114

Indianapolis Motor Speedway
4790 West 16th Street
Indianapolis, IN 46222

NASCAR
P.O. Box 2875
Daytona Beach, FL 32120

Internet Sites

Do you want to learn more about NASCAR trucks?
Visit the FACT HOUND at *http://www.facthound.com*

FACT HOUND can track down many sites to help you.
All the FACT HOUND sites are hand-selected by Capstone
Press editors. FACT HOUND will fetch the best, most accurate
information to answer your questions.

IT IS EASY! IT IS FUN!
1) Go to *http://www.facthound.com*
2) Type in: 0736815023
3) Click on "FETCH IT" and FACT HOUND will put you on
the trail of several helpful links.

**You can also search by subject or book title. So, relax
and let our pal FACT HOUND do the research for you!**

Index